Rise in Gratitude

A 12-WEEK CHALLENGE TO JOURNAL, REFLECT & GROW A GRATEFUL HEART

Sheila Chasse

CEO of Rise Fearlessly with Grit & Grace

Printed in the United States of America

Writing & Conceptualizing by Sheila Chasse

Proofreading, Copy Editing & Editorial Consulting by
Jennifer Karchmer

Cover Design & Interior Graphic Design by Jasleni Brito
JasleniDesigns.com

Fera Rose Photography by Heather Stein

More info at RiseFearlessly.com

This journal belongs to:

_____

Dedication

TO MY HUSBAND AND NUMBER ONE SUPPORTER JAMIE AND TO MY DEAREST CHILDREN, LOGAN, MASON, AND ROSELY:

It has been through my journeys with each of you that I have continued to grow in a life full of gratitude. I've learned through the best and hardest of times that a life lived in gratitude is one of the best gifts you can give yourself and the world. I want you to always have gratitude within you so let this journal be a guide for you to forever and always have it at your fingertips.

Practice gratitude every day. Think of it, pray on it, and if you lose sight of it, find your way back to it. Apply it to everything and most importantly, walk in it. Spread it. Make it an essential part of your life's foundation and you will experience life as the beautiful gift it is.

I am so grateful for you four. I love you with every part of my being in this world and beyond.

–Sheila Lynn Chasse,
CEO of Rise Fearlessly with Grit & Grace

I believe that one of the most powerful weapons we can use against our daily battles is finding the faith and courage to be grateful anyway—through the good times and tough times. Sometimes our paths can be difficult because we have a higher calling. You must shed any energy that does not match the frequency of your calling. This honors all that you are meant for and more, whether you know what that is or are still on your journey toward it.

Bring gratitude to your table. Pay attention to the things that light you up and always do so with a grateful heart as it's the magnet for miracles. Take up space and use your God-given voice. Express all the gratefulness for this journey and do something beautiful with it.

About the Author

Rise in Gratitude • Sheila Chasse

My name is Sheila Lynn Chasse and, first and foremost, I want to thank you for choosing this book and dedicating your time to it. It will be life-changing if you apply it every day in every way. A little bit about myself, I grew up in an exceedingly small farm town (my father a farmer himself) called Bascom, Ohio. In short, I had a tough childhood/early adulthood, but now I can say I am grateful for it because it helped shape me into the woman I am today. I fought so hard to become her! If you have not read my full story and would like to read more about my life and how I persevered despite many odds against me, you can do so on my website at RiseFearlessly.com.

Moving forward, at almost 21, I met my soulmate in 2008 while on Spring Break in Florida. Here I am, the small-town farmer's daughter from Ohio and then there he was, Jamie, the Connecticut man, who also happened to be on vacation in Florida for Daytona Bike Week 2008. To make a long and beautiful story short (so I don't end up turning this into an autobiography), we clicked! In that moment, the whole universe existed just to bring us together and I believe it was fate. Just two months after meeting, I moved to Connecticut, and today, 14 years after meeting and 7 years after our wedding, we have three beautiful children: Logan, Mason, and our newest, Rosely.

I'm just giving very small micro clips of my life here as it would be impossible to share every single detail that helped cultivate this book in such a short introduction. So much goes behind all of this and how gratitude became such a huge focus in my life. This is just the beginning of what I want to offer the world—leaving it a little better than I found it! All of life's circumstances can be teachers in disguise when we look through a grateful-hearted lens. Even if during those life struggles or circumstances, if we don't initially see the positive or can't feel the gratitude in the moment (which is totally normal when going through struggles), there is something to become of it after the fact. Something that can mold you for the better. Like for instance, I'm writing this book after many struggles and life's ups and downs, because through it all, I held on to what gratitude would lead me to and that is out of the darkness and into this light, a light that I am now sharing with you all!

From coming out the other side of having a parent with severe addiction, being diagnosed with cancer while pregnant with our first son, losing another son at 14 weeks pregnant before having our next son, to battling other health issues that arose after the fact, just the highs and lows of life. Losing loved ones, growing out of friendships for the better, battling through tough seasons, you know all of life's stuff and circumstances, we all have and go through this. But a steady thing through it all and how we overcame and still overcome, is the grateful heart we carry. Practicing gratitude can make going through all those things less painful, or healing from them easier. It plants the seed for more things to be grateful for and to come your way amongst the tough times and tough seasons. It is life-changing when you realize all that is in front of you that you still have to be grateful for despite the tough times. It reminds me of the Walt Whitman quote, "Keep your face always toward the sunshine, and the shadows will fall behind you." And let me just be cliché and say, if you cannot find that sunshine, create it! What I mean by that is what this book stands for. List what you are grateful for despite all the "shadows" you may be dealing with and watch how the sun peeks in and reminds you that this too shall pass, the sun is going to rise yet again and gratitude for that very feeling of knowing that can change your entire course. Today is a good day to have a good day because this is all we have, my friends—the present. Let the rays of gratitude touch every corner of your life and soak in the blessings that it shows you.

"GRATITUDE DOESN'T CHANGE THE SCENERY. IT MERELY WASHES CLEAN THE GLASS YOU LOOK THROUGH SO YOU CAN CLEARLY SEE THE COLORS."

-RICHELLE E. GOODRICH

About the Imagery

I would like to start off by sharing the reason I chose the imagery/flowers for this book because I am all about meaningful detail and everything I picked for my first daily devotional journal, I have personally created with meaning and purpose.

To start, the roses. Roses (especially pink) have always been a part of my life, especially growing up, and one of my favorite flowers. The pink rose symbolic meaning, which was even more fitting for this journal, is gratitude, grace, and joy. Overall, pink roses suggest gentleness. All shades of roses I grew up around, but the variety of pink roses I just remember being surrounded by. My father maintained and kept a beautiful rose garden while I was growing up as did his mother. Also, my mother's mother was a gardener and though I was not close to my extended family, roses felt like a connection to us all. Growing up, my dad would cut fresh flowers and bring them to me and that was one of his ways of showing his love for me. As an adult, my love for roses continued and they were a part of our wedding. They are the flower my husband has always gotten for me to show sweet gestures of love. We also started our own rose garden area at our home for our kids to enjoy, and it has just been a continuous tradition we've carried on this beautiful journey of life. And now, our daughter, born in May 2021, was named Rosely after a beautiful pink rose. So having the roses in the imagery in this book was even more honorary for our daughter. She has added so much joy into our lives.

In this journal, you will also notice hydrangeas. I did not have a constant motherly figure in my life growing up. I did have a few women step up to the plate and help where they could and for that I am so grateful. It was not until I met my husband in 2008, and when I met his mother, Claudette, who became my mother-in-law, that I would have the chance to experience a constant motherly figure. I love Claudette and will always admire her for being the strong, courageous, and constant motherly figure in my life—longer than I ever had. I admire her for raising such an amazing man whom I am so blessed to call my soulmate, and for building the family she built and the legacy we will carry on in her memory. We lost her very unexpectedly in February 2020. Hydrangeas remind me of her as she grew the most beautiful ones in her yard. Claudette always had them cut and placed in vases around her house and would bring me some to put in my house as well. When I spent several days in the hospital a year before she passed, she cut me the most beautiful blue hydrangea to sit in my hospital room. I still have the photo I took of that flower sitting next to me by my hospital bed during a very tough time, brightening up my room/day as we waited for so many answers during that hospital stay. So, when looking up the meaning to tie hydrangeas into this book, it was like they were meant to add to my roses as hydrangeas symbolize gratitude, grace, and beauty—almost identical to our pink rose symbolic meaning. Hydrangeas also symbolize love, harmony, and peace. When I see hydrangeas, I like to be reminded of the peace I know Claudette feels in heaven and her love that we still feel all around us that she left with us.

Marigolds are another beautiful flower you will notice in this journal and those represent my two sons: Logan, born in October 2015 and Mason, born in October 2018. Marigolds are their birth month flower, and they are also a flower we plant every year around our back deck. With their bright colors, marigolds are said to represent the beauty and warmth of the rising sun, reminding us that even the darkest nights will end, and the sun will rise again. This is what my boys have given us. Through the toughest times, their pure and innocent hearts give such unconditional love even on the tough Mommin' days we all experience. They still are the sunshine on cloudy days that brightens our life and world.

I want to leave you with this beautiful quote that I feel summarizes how flowers are just like us in this circle of life.

"THIS IS THE RECIPE OF LIFE SAID MY MOTHER AS SHE HELD ME IN HER ARMS AS I WEPT. THINK OF THOSE FLOWERS YOU PLANT IN THE GARDEN EACH YEAR, THEY WILL TEACH YOU THAT PEOPLE TOO MUST WILT, FALL, ROOT, RISE, IN ORDER TO BLOOM." - RUPI KAUR

Why Gratitude?

We can do all the "things." Eat clean, drink our H20, exercise, listen to motivational speakers, meditate, give ourselves what we consider self-care, whatever taking care of you looks like, but so many of us forget one simple step and that is feeding our mindset in a healthy manner so we can do the "things" in a better more gratifying state. There is no better place to start to get your mind in good health than with gratitude. It is essential and though many say they are grateful for things and have all the gratitude decor around the house, how many people are intentionally practicing gratitude? We can be in such a constant state of rushing that it can be so hard to see and absorb the wonderful gifts that surround us.

It is life-changing to start intentionally practicing gratitude. I know it helped me during some of the scariest, uncertain times of my life. My gratitude journey (when I consciously started practicing it) began back in 2014, right before I was diagnosed with cancer at 17 weeks pregnant with our first son. At this point in my life at the age of 27, I knew what gratitude was of course, but never practiced it daily or even applied it to daily living. So, after picking up a daily gratitude journal, I started my own journey with gratitude and applying it intentionally to my life and as a result, everything began to change all around me. Despite getting the news that I had cancer in the middle of this gratitude journey I was on, it was gratitude (and my faith) that helped get me through.

When I could have lost my mind with all the fear, anxiety, worry— you name it—I leaned deeply into my gratitude. Though things were going crazy all around me during this season of my life, things also kept changing for the better. Chemotherapy was doing its job and removing the cancer, my pregnancy was going as smooth as possible for undergoing the cancer treatments while pregnant, yet life still felt like an amazing blessing despite all the bumps we were hitting and going over. I never felt "Why me?" because I knew all that I still had to be grateful for, but I would not have been able to maintain such an attitude without intentionally applying gratitude to my life each day. Fear, anxiety, worry, these can all slip in so easily and take over your mindset, paralyze you to the point you cannot even focus on gratitude or, better yet, witness it in your life. I have been there. Gratitude was and still is my anchor. There are other things, but gratitude sets the foundation for me to "keep on keeping on." It is the roots that keep me grounded in all that I have, all that is around me, all that is or was, to remind me daily to be thankful even during the hard or challenging times. It will keep you going, in a healthy manner—when a tornado of emotions wants to get the best of us.

Going back briefly to my beginning journey with gratitude while simultaneously being diagnosed with cancer—the two really went into play together because despite the cancer, I was growing life inside of me. Talk about GRATITUDE!! Something may have been trying to take life from me (cancer), but I was not allowing it to rob me of living it gratefully, especially for the life I was about to bring into the world. How could I not feel the gratitude in the situation? So, this is just one prime example of how gratitude played a huge role in my journey and how it continues to do so daily. When you stop to "smell the roses," you will witness the beauty and feel the gratitude all around you. Just remember this all has to be an intentional practice because with the craziness of life, we can forget the basics and where happiness truly lies. Like I stated in the beginning, we can do all the "things," but starting with your mindset is the key to propel you into a state of true joy and happiness, a place you don't feel you need to run from.

The Purpose of Gratitude

We all know what gratitude means and we all practice it in different ways, but to be fully intentionally grateful takes work. By this I mean to see FULLY what you have and NOT what you are missing. It is when you keep the focus zoomed in on your gifts, not your lack of. This will require you to keep your mindset on the right things and sometimes you will have to really work at that making it extremely intentional which is where that "work" comes in. It is so easy to let our minds go in the opposite direction and think of all that we are lacking, missing, needing, or wishing for which takes all the things we could be currently grateful for and tucks them away. We miss the blessings. We miss the purpose of life itself when we live in that kind of state of mind, not to mention the anxiety and depression that can arise because of that way of thinking. So, just like anything you are learning or trying to achieve, consistency with practicing gratitude is where the magic will happen. Literally day by day, again and again, as you practice gratitude, life will start looking a whole lot different and you will reap the amazing benefits of that all around. If you are stuck right now in life or in a certain situation or difficulties have arisen in your life and who knows how long you will have to walk that road, having gratitude in your "mental toolbox" can help you renew your mind and make it through those tough times so much easier. Gratitude can help make that unknown, difficult road manageable. You become hopeful in that fact that you have so much else around you to be thankful for. Just having the sight to see and the ability to read these very words is something to be grateful for. Noticing those little blessings amongst the hard times in your life can bring a light back into your life that helps you to "keep on keeping on."

GRATITUDE SHOULD NOT BE JUST A REACTION TO GETTING WHAT YOU WANT, BUT AN ALL-THE-TIME GRATITUDE, THE KIND WHERE YOU NOTICE THE LITTLE THINGS AND WHERE YOU CONSTANTLY LOOK FOR GOOD, EVEN IN UNPLEASANT SITUATIONS. START BRINGING GRATITUDE TO YOUR EXPERIENCES, INSTEAD OF WAITING FOR A POSITIVE EXPERIENCE IN ORDER TO FEEL GRATEFUL.

- MARELISA FABREGA

How to use this Journal

I cannot say it enough: gratitude—expressing it and surrounding yourself with it—is truly life-changing. But living in a world full of busyness, neglect, and doubt can make it hard to find or focus on gratitude so we must be INTENTIONAL with practicing it. Just like taking a daily vitamin, make gratitude part of your morning routine. Gratitude must be taken daily and intentionally applied as it's a natural way to improve our mental and physical health. So, this journal is intended to help you be intentional with your gratitude, to help guide you on the journey if practicing gratitude daily is new to you. This practice will help thankfulness flourish in your life and expand your heart to places you did not even know it could be expanded to.

Each day for the next 12 weeks, you will find 5 simple steps to fill out and follow each morning before turning on any electronics or checking your phone. This process and these steps will help set the tone for your day. The purpose of this practice is to recognize the good that is already there amongst the daily stress or trials you may be currently experiencing. You will be able to put all of your racing thoughts in a place (this journal) where they can work in your favor and bring you abundance instead of more stress. Remember, thoughts become THINGS. If we can set the right thoughts in our minds and start to actually believe them, we can hold whatever it may be in our hands.

First off, you will notice at the start of each week, there is a place to write out your top 3 important To Do's as this is another helper in cleaning out our mind space before pouring in all the gratitude that will follow on the next page.

Next, you will find the first step in the 5 steps that you will complete each morning starts with your **GRATITUDE LIST**. You will write 5 things you are grateful for and end with "because." Adding "because" to anything you are grateful for will make you think about WHY you are grateful for it. Just to simply state you are grateful for X,Y & Z, only gives half the story. To unleash the full power of gratitude, you must know WHY you are grateful for it.

Rise in Gratitude • Sheila Chasse

The 5 things you are grateful for will change day to day of course. Here's an example that I wrote recently: "I am grateful for my sight because it allows me to see the faces of those I love and the beauty of this world."

Next, I ask what your **VISION** for the day is. Not for your week or for the following day, but the present day and moment. The present is all that we currently have and where we should keep our mind. The Now. Ask yourself, "What would make today GREAT?!" Remember, Thoughts Become Things!

After Vision comes your **INTENTIONS** for the day. What will you do, what will you aim for? What do you commit yourself to today? Remember that intentions remind our mind, hearts, and soul of our desires for the day. Intentions are in the PRESENT MOMENT and are independent of achieving a goal or destination. Intentions do however support our goals by setting them daily because they serve as a road map and reminder on how to live each day with intention. Here's another example: "Today, I commit myself to healthy eating." Your intention is to eat healthy because maybe your goal is to get into good physical health. Intentions are building blocks that help support our goals!

MAKE SPACE comes next. Make space for the new by jotting down all you may be carrying. Unload it all in that spot. You are not created to carry so much weight. If you are not speaking it, you are storing it, and that gets heavy. Do not even try to make sense of all you write. Do not judge it. Let it flow. We need to declutter our minds just like decluttering a closet or crowded space. Making space for better things means more room for growth, like our gratitude!

Lastly, **RELEASE**! What can you simply LET GO OF and LET BE? Or if you are the religious type, you can "Let go and let God." Release things that have created a negative attachment. Toxic thoughts, emotions, anything that does not serve you or is not propelling you into the right direction can go, especially if it is something that is out of your hands because it deserves the freedom from your mind too. Let this be your beginning to something so life-changing! As you complete these daily, repetitive steps each morning, watch how you will steadily grow a more grateful heart and a faith in yourself that will strengthen and deepen and inspire all of those around you. Living your so-called "Best Life" starts from within. No number of things will get you your best life if you are internally suffering. Let us rise up in gratitude and watch our best self appear and in return our best life can be fully lived AND appreciated for what it is. Do not just go through life on auto-pilot, which causes you to miss so much.

WEEK 1

"GOOD DAYS" START WITH

Gratitude

It is as simple as that! When our days are started in a mindset of gratitude, happiness comes far more easily even on those tough days because you are reminded of all the blessings in your life.

We all get caught up in the daily push-and-pull of life and our "To Do's" and so forth, which can cause us to easily forget the blessings we have all around us. So, when we direct our minds to gratitude, those vibrations you are putting out into the world/universe can cause better circumstances, events, and the abundance you desire to be attracted to you like a magnet—not to mention starting your day with gratitude literally sets the tone for the rest of your day and will increase your productivity immensely. It will change your entire outlook for your day and ground you into a sense of peace that, even if interrupted with life's hiccups, you can place yourself back into that peace very easily. Being thankful for the day you are in and given can shed any negativity you are carrying around and open yourself up to the positive side of life.

Always keep in mind that a beautiful day begins with a beautiful mindset and the root of that is gratitude. Start there and watch the rest unfold.

HERE IS TO A NEW WEEK AHEAD! EACH WEEK WE START OFF WITH THIS!

The life you want is on the other side of that "stuff" you do not want to do. You have a whole new week ahead of you and though we cannot know what will be in store for us, we can start with a grateful heart and utilize the time we so graciously have been given. With that being said, use the space below to jot down what you aim to accomplish or tackle in the week to come. Do not overwhelm yourself with a huge To-Do List as too much listed is not a good thing. Keep it short and attainable, setting realistic goals.

List 3 things that would help you feel a sense of clarity and accomplishment if you completed them this week.

Make it a practical list of attainable goals so you can check off small wins this week. Instead of an overwhelming project like, "Clean out the garage" try, "Put kids' summer toys in big gray bin and store under the stairs." Remember, it's "progress, not perfection."

To Do's

1.

2.

3.

DATE: ___/___/_____

GRATITUDE » I am grateful for....
(write what you are grateful for and because)

1. _____
   _____

2. _____
   _____

3. _____
   _____

4. _____
   _____

5. _____
   _____

VISION » What would make today great?

_____

_____

_____

_____

_____

_____

Rise in Gratitude • Sheila Chasse

INTENTIONS » Today, I commit myself to....

_____

_____

_____

_____

MAKE SPACE » What is on my mind, in my heart, or on my shoulders?

_____

_____

_____

_____

RELEASE » Let go of....

_____

_____

_____

_____

"When gratitude becomes an essential foundation in our lives, miracles start to appear everywhere."

- Emmanuel Dagher

DATE: ___/___/_____

GRATITUDE » I am grateful for....
(write what you are grateful for and because)

1. _____

   _____

2. _____

   _____

3. _____

   _____

4. _____

   _____

5. _____

   _____

VISION » What would make today great?

_____

_____

_____

_____

_____

_____

Rise in Gratitude • Sheila Chasse

INTENTIONS » Today, I commit myself to....

_____

_____

_____

_____

MAKE SPACE » What is on my mind, in my heart, or on my shoulders?

_____

_____

_____

_____

RELEASE » Let go of....

_____

_____

_____

_____

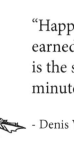

"Happiness cannot be traveled to, owned, earned, worn, or consumed. Happiness is the spiritual experience of living every minute with love, grace, and gratitude."

- Denis Waitley

DATE: ___/___/_____

GRATITUDE » I am grateful for....
(write what you are grateful for and because)

1. _____
   _____

2. _____
   _____

3. _____
   _____

4. _____
   _____

5. _____
   _____

VISION » What would make today great?

_____

_____

_____

_____

_____

Rise in Gratitude • Sheila Chasse

INTENTIONS » Today, I commit myself to....

_____

_____

_____

_____

MAKE SPACE » What is on my mind, in my heart, or on my shoulders?

_____

_____

_____

_____

RELEASE » Let go of....

_____

_____

_____

_____

"Gratitude helps you see what is there instead of what isn't."

- Unknown

DATE: ___/___/_____

GRATITUDE » I am grateful for....
(write what you are grateful for and because)

1. _____
   _____

2. _____
   _____

3. _____
   _____

4. _____
   _____

5. _____
   _____

VISION » What would make today great?

_____

_____

_____

_____

_____

_____

Rise in Gratitude • Sheila Chasse

INTENTIONS » Today, I commit myself to....

_____

_____

_____

_____

MAKE SPACE » What is on my mind, in my heart, or on my shoulders?

_____

_____

_____

_____

RELEASE » Let go of....

_____

_____

_____

_____

"If you are not grateful for what you already have, what makes you think you would be happy with more?"

- Roy T. Bennett

DATE: ___/___/_____

GRATITUDE » I am grateful for....
(write what you are grateful for and because)

1. _____
   _____

2. _____
   _____

3. _____
   _____

4. _____
   _____

5. _____
   _____

VISION » What would make today great?

_____

_____

_____

_____

_____

_____

Rise in Gratitude • Sheila Chasse

INTENTIONS » Today, I commit myself to....

_____

_____

_____

_____

MAKE SPACE » What is on my mind, in my heart, or on my shoulders?

_____

_____

_____

_____

RELEASE » Let go of....

_____

_____

_____

_____

"Gratitude will shift you to a higher frequency, and you will attract much better things."

- Rhonda Byrne

DATE: ___/___/_____

GRATITUDE » I am grateful for....
(write what you are grateful for and because)

1. _____

   _____

2. _____

   _____

3. _____

   _____

4. _____

   _____

5. _____

   _____

VISION » What would make today great?

_____

_____

_____

_____

_____

_____

Rise in Gratitude • Sheila Chasse

INTENTIONS » Today, I commit myself to….

_____

_____

_____

_____

MAKE SPACE » What is on my mind, in my heart, or on my shoulders?

_____

_____

_____

_____

RELEASE » Let go of….

_____

_____

_____

_____

"When we focus on our gratitude, the tide of disappointment goes out, and the tide of love rushes in."

- Kristin Armstrong

DATE: ___/___/_____

GRATITUDE » I am grateful for....
(write what you are grateful for and because)

1. _____

   _____

2. _____

   _____

3. _____

   _____

4. _____

   _____

5. _____

   _____

VISION » What would make today great?

_____

_____

_____

_____

_____

_____

INTENTIONS » Today, I commit myself to....

_____

_____

_____

_____

MAKE SPACE » What is on my mind, in my heart, or on my shoulders?

_____

_____

_____

_____

RELEASE » Let go of....

_____

_____

_____

_____

"The more you are in a state of gratitude, the more you will attract things to be grateful for."

- Unknown

Gratitude
GUARDS YOUR HEART AGAINST GRUMBLING

What we focus on can make us either happy or simply put, miserable. We can either dwell on the negative things and grumble about it all or choose to magnify the good. When we stop and apply gratitude consciously when we are being negative or grumbling, gratitude can literally overtake the situation and guard our hearts from traveling down a negativity spiral. When we choose to be thankful, it releases a new level of faith, hope, and joy and this guards our hearts. We become happier and we bring more joy to those around us. Our energy can be felt, and boy can it change the world of many when we share that energy and light we have beaming inside of a grateful heart.

Amplify your gratitude and mute your grumbling and watch the growth occur.

HERE IS TO A NEW WEEK AHEAD! EACH WEEK WE START OFF WITH THIS!

The life you want is on the other side of that "stuff" you do not want to do. You have a whole new week ahead of you and though we cannot know what will be in store for us, we can start with a grateful heart and utilize the time we so graciously have been given. With that being said, use the space below to jot down what you aim to accomplish or tackle in the week to come. Do not overwhelm yourself with a huge To-Do List as too much listed is not a good thing. Keep it short and attainable, setting realistic goals.

List 3 things that would help you feel a sense of clarity and accomplishment if you completed them this week.

Make it a practical list of attainable goals so you can check off small wins this week. Instead of an overwhelming project like, "Clean out the garage" try, "Put kids' summer toys in big gray bin and store under the stairs." Remember, it's "progress, not perfection."

To Do's

1.

2.

3.

DATE: ___/___/_____

GRATITUDE » I am grateful for....
(write what you are grateful for and because)

1. _____

   _____

2. _____

   _____

3. _____

   _____

4. _____

   _____

5. _____

   _____

VISION » What would make today great?

_____

_____

_____

_____

_____

_____

Rise in Gratitude • Sheila Chasse

INTENTIONS » Today, I commit myself to....

_____

_____

_____

_____

MAKE SPACE » What is on my mind, in my heart, or on my shoulders?

_____

_____

_____

_____

RELEASE » Let go of....

_____

_____

_____

_____

"Gratitude is an essential part of being present. When you go deeply into the present, gratitude arises spontaneously."

- Eckhart Tolle

DATE: ___/___/_____

GRATITUDE » I am grateful for....
(write what you are grateful for and because)

1. _____
   _____

2. _____
   _____

3. _____
   _____

4. _____
   _____

5. _____
   _____

VISION » What would make today great?

_____

_____

_____

_____

_____

Rise in Gratitude • Sheila Chasse

INTENTIONS » Today, I commit myself to....

_____

_____

_____

_____

MAKE SPACE » What is on my mind, in my heart, or on my shoulders?

_____

_____

_____

_____

RELEASE » Let go of....

_____

_____

_____

_____

"Gratitude helps you fall in love with the life you already have."

- Unknown

DATE: ___/___/_____

GRATITUDE » I am grateful for....
(write what you are grateful for and because)

1. _____

   _____

2. _____

   _____

3. _____

   _____

4. _____

   _____

5. _____

   _____

VISION » What would make today great?

_____

_____

_____

_____

_____

_____

Rise in Gratitude • Sheila Chasse

INTENTIONS » Today, I commit myself to....

_____

_____

_____

_____

MAKE SPACE » What is on my mind, in my heart, or on my shoulders?

_____

_____

_____

_____

RELEASE » Let go of....

_____

_____

_____

_____

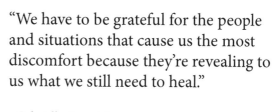

"We have to be grateful for the people and situations that cause us the most discomfort because they're revealing to us what we still need to heal."

- Gabrielle Bernstein

DATE: ___/___/_____

GRATITUDE » I am grateful for....
(write what you are grateful for and because)

1. _____
   _____

2. _____
   _____

3. _____
   _____

4. _____
   _____

5. _____
   _____

VISION » What would make today great?

_____

_____

_____

_____

_____

_____

Rise in Gratitude • Sheila Chasse

INTENTIONS » Today, I commit myself to....

_____

_____

_____

_____

MAKE SPACE » What is on my mind, in my heart, or on my shoulders?

_____

_____

_____

_____

RELEASE » Let go of....

_____

_____

_____

_____

"When gratitude becomes your default setting, life changes."

- Nancy Leigh DeMoss

DATE: ___/___/_____

GRATITUDE » I am grateful for....
(write what you are grateful for and because)

1. _____

   _____

2. _____

   _____

3. _____

   _____

4. _____

   _____

5. _____

   _____

VISION » What would make today great?

_____

_____

_____

_____

_____

_____

Rise in Gratitude • Sheila Chasse

INTENTIONS » Today, I commit myself to....

_____

_____

_____

_____

MAKE SPACE » What is on my mind, in my heart, or on my shoulders?

_____

_____

_____

_____

RELEASE » Let go of....

_____

_____

_____

_____

"We forget that waking up each day is the first thing we should be grateful for."

- Unknown

DATE: ___/___/_____

GRATITUDE » I am grateful for....
(write what you are grateful for and because)

1. _____
   _____

2. _____
   _____

3. _____
   _____

4. _____
   _____

5. _____
   _____

VISION » What would make today great?

_____
_____
_____
_____
_____
_____

Rise in Gratitude • Sheila Chasse

INTENTIONS » Today, I commit myself to....

_____

_____

_____

_____

MAKE SPACE » What is on my mind, in my heart, or on my shoulders?

_____

_____

_____

_____

RELEASE » Let go of....

_____

_____

_____

_____

"If you want to find happiness,
find gratitude."

- Steve Maraboli

DATE: ___/___/_____

GRATITUDE » I am grateful for....
(write what you are grateful for and because)

1. _____
   _____

2. _____
   _____

3. _____
   _____

4. _____
   _____

5. _____
   _____

VISION » What would make today great?

_____

_____

_____

_____

_____

Rise in Gratitude • Sheila Chasse

INTENTIONS » Today, I commit myself to….

_____

_____

_____

_____

MAKE SPACE » What is on my mind, in my heart, or on my shoulders?

_____

_____

_____

_____

RELEASE » Let go of….

_____

_____

_____

_____

"The real gift of gratitude is that the more grateful you are, the more present you become."

- Dr. Robert Holden

WHY IS

Gratitude

THE ATTITUDE?

If you had to choose an attitude to have, gratitude should be it or at least an amazing starting point! Why? Because having an attitude of gratitude means you are operating from a place of abundance instead of a place of scarcity or fear and operating from a place of abundance is only going to attract far better things to you. You can stand in your own way and even block blessings trying to come to you by having an attitude of ungratefulness. Gratitude is simply the attitude that will determine your altitude, how far you will go. If you are asking God or whomever you pray to for a breakthrough, you must start thanking your higher power first before that breakthrough. We do not (usually) get the breakthrough first. So, having gratitude as your attitude amongst the dust and debris you may be working through, will determine the altitude in which you will reach past all of that. It will determine how you come out on the other side.

Gratitude is the best attitude that takes us to the next altitude and helps us live our best lives by truly seeing the blessings from the dust we pushed through to the sky never being our limit as we have painted it in our own gratefulness, which makes anything possible and one hell of an attitude to share with the world!

HERE IS TO A NEW WEEK AHEAD! EACH WEEK WE START OFF WITH THIS!

The life you want is on the other side of that "stuff" you do not want to do. You have a whole new week ahead of you and though we cannot know what will be in store for us, we can start with a grateful heart and utilize the time we so graciously have been given. With that being said, use the space below to jot down what you aim to accomplish or tackle in the week to come. Do not overwhelm yourself with a huge To-Do List as too much listed is not a good thing. Keep it short and attainable, setting realistic goals.

List 3 things that would help you feel a sense of clarity and accomplishment if you completed them this week.

Make it a practical list of attainable goals so you can check off small wins this week. Instead of an overwhelming project like, "Clean out the garage" try, "Put kids' summer toys in big gray bin and store under the stairs." Remember, it's "progress, not perfection."

To Do's

1.

2.

3.

DATE: ___/___/_____

GRATITUDE » I am grateful for....
(write what you are grateful for and because)

1. _____

   _____

2. _____

   _____

3. _____

   _____

4. _____

   _____

5. _____

   _____

VISION » What would make today great?

_____

_____

_____

_____

_____

_____

INTENTIONS » Today, I commit myself to….

_____

_____

_____

_____

MAKE SPACE » What is on my mind, in my heart, or on my shoulders?

_____

_____

_____

_____

RELEASE » Let go of….

_____

_____

_____

_____

"It is not happiness that brings us gratitude. It is gratitude that brings us happiness."

- Anonymous

DATE: ___/___/_____

GRATITUDE » I am grateful for....
(write what you are grateful for and because)

1. _____
   _____

2. _____
   _____

3. _____
   _____

4. _____
   _____

5. _____
   _____

VISION » What would make today great?

_____

_____

_____

_____

_____

Rise in Gratitude • Sheila Chasse

INTENTIONS » Today, I commit myself to....

_____

_____

_____

_____

MAKE SPACE » What is on my mind, in my heart, or on my shoulders?

_____

_____

_____

_____

RELEASE » Let go of....

_____

_____

_____

_____

"The more you are in a state of gratitude, the more you will attract things to be grateful for."

- Walt Disney

DATE: ___/___/_____

GRATITUDE » I am grateful for....
(write what you are grateful for and because)

1. _____

   _____

2. _____

   _____

3. _____

   _____

4. _____

   _____

5. _____

   _____

VISION » What would make today great?

_____

_____

_____

_____

_____

_____

Rise in Gratitude • Sheila Chasse

INTENTIONS » Today, I commit myself to....

_____

_____

_____

_____

MAKE SPACE » What is on my mind, in my heart, or on my shoulders?

_____

_____

_____

_____

RELEASE » Let go of....

_____

_____

_____

_____

"The root of joy is gratefulness."

- David Steindl-Rast

DATE: ___/___/_____

GRATITUDE » I am grateful for....
(write what you are grateful for and because)

1. _____
   _____

2. _____
   _____

3. _____
   _____

4. _____
   _____

5. _____
   _____

VISION » What would make today great?

_____

_____

_____

_____

_____

_____

Rise in Gratitude • Sheila Chasse

INTENTIONS » Today, I commit myself to....

_____

_____

_____

_____

MAKE SPACE » What is on my mind, in my heart, or on my shoulders?

_____

_____

_____

_____

RELEASE » Let go of....

_____

_____

_____

_____

"Gratitude blocks toxic emotions such as envy, resentment, regret and depression, which can destroy our happiness. It is impossible to feel envious and grateful at the same time."

- Robert Emmons

DATE: ___/___/_____

GRATITUDE » I am grateful for....
(write what you are grateful for and because)

1. _____

    _____

2. _____

    _____

3. _____

    _____

4. _____

    _____

5. _____

    _____

VISION » What would make today great?

_____

_____

_____

_____

_____

_____

Rise in Gratitude • Sheila Chasse

INTENTIONS » Today, I commit myself to....

_____

_____

_____

_____

MAKE SPACE » What is on my mind, in my heart, or on my shoulders?

_____

_____

_____

_____

RELEASE » Let go of....

_____

_____

_____

_____

"There is a calmness to a life lived in gratitude, a quiet joy."

- Ralph H. Blum

DATE: ___/___/_____

GRATITUDE » I am grateful for....
(write what you are grateful for and because)

1. _____
   _____

2. _____
   _____

3. _____
   _____

4. _____
   _____

5. _____
   _____

VISION » What would make today great?

_____
_____
_____
_____
_____
_____

Rise in Gratitude • Sheila Chasse

INTENTIONS » Today, I commit myself to....

_____

_____

_____

_____

MAKE SPACE » What is on my mind, in my heart, or on my shoulders?

_____

_____

_____

_____

RELEASE » Let go of....

_____

_____

_____

_____

"You simply will not be the same person two months from now after consciously giving thanks each day for the abundance that exists in your life. And you will have set in motion an ancient spiritual law; the more you have and are grateful for, the more will be given to you."

- Sarah Ban Breathnach

DATE: ___/___/_____

GRATITUDE » I am grateful for....
(write what you are grateful for and because)

1. _____

_____

2. _____

_____

3. _____

_____

4. _____

_____

5. _____

_____

VISION » What would make today great?

_____

_____

_____

_____

_____

_____

Rise in Gratitude • Sheila Chasse

INTENTIONS » Today, I commit myself to....

_____

_____

_____

_____

MAKE SPACE » What is on my mind, in my heart, or on my shoulders?

_____

_____

_____

_____

RELEASE » Let go of....

_____

_____

_____

_____

"The miracle of gratitude is that it shifts your perception to such an extent that it changes the world you see."

- Dr. Robert Holden

Gratitude
IS THE NEUTRALIZER OF ENVY

Envy. It can sneak up on you and give you the pesky desire to think you need what someone else has. Social media is a prime example and how scrolling through people's highlight reel posts (showing mostly the good times only) can easily get your mind into a place of envy or wishing your life were more like theirs. Little do we know of the in-betweens (aka, real life) of their photos and maybe the unhappiness or pain they really are experiencing, but not sharing. So, envy invades our hearts and steals our joy over a simple snippet off social media that is not the full story, usually.

Envy can also look like sorrow over a door being closed to us but opened to a friend or associate. It even can creep in as disappointment when we think someone else has better-behaved kids for example or is more actively fit and healthier (from what they share) than us, the list goes on. No matter what, we can be sure we are dealing with envy when we notice feelings of anger, resentment, or even competition with others. And this my friend is where gratitude can step in and SAVE THE DAY!

Gratitude blocks those toxic emotions such as envy, resentment, and anger and gratitude helps us stop fueling our need to compete or "Be like the Joneses" and keeps us from destroying our own happiness. When we realize our joy and contentment is not found in our circumstances or in someone else's for that matter, we have a heart at peace, and it is anchored in far more than just the number of friends we have or possessions we own. The battle in the mind will end where gratitude begins.

Just remember, it is impossible to feel envious and grateful at the same time. So, when at a crossroads, pick the higher road and better serving road (gratitude) for your own personal well-being, and watch how your happiness goes uninterrupted.

HERE IS TO A NEW WEEK AHEAD! EACH WEEK WE START OFF WITH THIS!

The life you want is on the other side of that "stuff" you do not want to do. You have a whole new week ahead of you and though we cannot know what will be in store for us, we can start with a grateful heart and utilize the time we so graciously have been given. With that being said, use the space below to jot down what you aim to accomplish or tackle in the week to come. Do not overwhelm yourself with a huge To-Do List as too much listed is not a good thing. Keep it short and attainable, setting realistic goals.

List 3 things that would help you feel a sense of clarity and accomplishment if you completed them this week.

Make it a practical list of attainable goals so you can check off small wins this week. Instead of an overwhelming project like, "Clean out the garage" try, "Put kids' summer toys in big gray bin and store under the stairs." Remember, it's "progress, not perfection."

To Do's

1.

2.

3.

DATE: ___/___/_____

GRATITUDE » I am grateful for....
(write what you are grateful for and because)

1. _____
   _____

2. _____
   _____

3. _____
   _____

4. _____
   _____

5. _____
   _____

VISION » What would make today great?

_____
_____
_____
_____
_____
_____

Rise in Gratitude • Sheila Chasse

INTENTIONS » Today, I commit myself to....

_____

_____

_____

_____

MAKE SPACE » What is on my mind, in my heart, or on my shoulders?

_____

_____

_____

_____

RELEASE » Let go of....

_____

_____

_____

_____

"The most powerful weapon against your daily battles is finding the courage to be grateful anyway."

- Anonymous

DATE: ___/___/_____

GRATITUDE » I am grateful for....
(write what you are grateful for and because)

1. _____

   _____

2. _____

   _____

3. _____

   _____

4. _____

   _____

5. _____

   _____

VISION » What would make today great?

_____

_____

_____

_____

_____

_____

Rise in Gratitude • Sheila Chasse

INTENTIONS » Today, I commit myself to....

_____

_____

_____

_____

MAKE SPACE » What is on my mind, in my heart, or on my shoulders?

_____

_____

_____

_____

RELEASE » Let go of....

_____

_____

_____

_____

"Gratitude makes everything grow."

- Mary Davis

DATE: ___/___/_____

GRATITUDE » I am grateful for....
(write what you are grateful for and because)

1. _____

   _____

2. _____

   _____

3. _____

   _____

4. _____

   _____

5. _____

   _____

VISION » What would make today great?

_____

_____

_____

_____

_____

Rise in Gratitude • Sheila Chasse

INTENTIONS » Today, I commit myself to....

_____

_____

_____

_____

MAKE SPACE » What is on my mind, in my heart, or on my shoulders?

_____

_____

_____

_____

RELEASE » Let go of....

_____

_____

_____

_____

"The struggle ends when the gratitude begins."

- Neale Donald Walsch

DATE: ___/___/_____

GRATITUDE » I am grateful for....
(write what you are grateful for and because)

1. _____

_____

2. _____

_____

3. _____

_____

4. _____

_____

5. _____

_____

VISION » What would make today great?

_____

_____

_____

_____

_____

_____

INTENTIONS » Today, I commit myself to....

_____

_____

_____

_____

MAKE SPACE » What is on my mind, in my heart, or on my shoulders?

_____

_____

_____

_____

RELEASE » Let go of....

_____

_____

_____

_____

"When you are grateful, fear disappears, and abundance appears."

- Tony Robbins

DATE: ___/___/_____

GRATITUDE » I am grateful for....
(write what you are grateful for and because)

1. _____

   _____

2. _____

   _____

3. _____

   _____

4. _____

   _____

5. _____

   _____

VISION » What would make today great?

_____

_____

_____

_____

_____

_____

Rise in Gratitude • Sheila Chasse

INTENTIONS » Today, I commit myself to....

_____

_____

_____

_____

MAKE SPACE » What is on my mind, in my heart, or on my shoulders?

_____

_____

_____

_____

RELEASE » Let go of....

_____

_____

_____

_____

"Interrupt anxiety with gratitude."

- Anonymous

DATE: ___/___/_____

GRATITUDE » I am grateful for....
(write what you are grateful for and because)

1. _____
   _____

2. _____
   _____

3. _____
   _____

4. _____
   _____

5. _____
   _____

VISION » What would make today great?

_____

_____

_____

_____

_____

_____

Rise in Gratitude • Sheila Chasse

INTENTIONS » Today, I commit myself to....

_____

_____

_____

_____

MAKE SPACE » What is on my mind, in my heart, or on my shoulders?

_____

_____

_____

_____

RELEASE » Let go of....

_____

_____

_____

_____

"Gratitude is an opener of locked-up blessings."

- Marianne Williamson

DATE: ___/___/_____

GRATITUDE » I am grateful for....
(write what you are grateful for and because)

1. _____
_____

2. _____
_____

3. _____
_____

4. _____
_____

5. _____
_____

VISION » What would make today great?

_____

_____

_____

_____

_____

_____

Rise in Gratitude • Sheila Chasse

INTENTIONS » Today, I commit myself to....

_____

_____

_____

_____

MAKE SPACE » What is on my mind, in my heart, or on my shoulders?

_____

_____

_____

_____

RELEASE » Let go of....

_____

_____

_____

_____

"Gratitude is the single most
important ingredient to living
a successful and fulfilled life."

- Jack Canfield

KEEP GOING AND
Keep Growing

"All your experiences have been preparing you for your current lessons. Every past triumph and trail have equipped you for this very moment. Move past your current situation with grace and call on the strength you have developed within. The reward will be more significant than you could even imagine. Keep going. You've Got This."

– @commandinglife

HERE IS TO A NEW WEEK AHEAD! EACH WEEK WE START OFF WITH THIS!

The life you want is on the other side of that "stuff" you do not want to do. You have a whole new week ahead of you and though we cannot know what will be in store for us, we can start with a grateful heart and utilize the time we so graciously have been given. With that being said, use the space below to jot down what you aim to accomplish or tackle in the week to come. Do not overwhelm yourself with a huge To-Do List as too much listed is not a good thing. Keep it short and attainable, setting realistic goals.

List 3 things that would help you feel a sense of clarity and accomplishment if you completed them this week.

Make it a practical list of attainable goals so you can check off small wins this week. Instead of an overwhelming project like, "Clean out the garage" try, "Put kids' summer toys in big gray bin and store under the stairs." Remember, it's "progress, not perfection."

To Do's

1.

2.

3.

DATE: ___/___/_____

GRATITUDE » I am grateful for....
(write what you are grateful for and because)

1. _____
   _____

2. _____
   _____

3. _____
   _____

4. _____
   _____

5. _____
   _____

VISION » What would make today great?

_____

_____

_____

_____

_____

_____

Rise in Gratitude • Sheila Chasse

INTENTIONS » Today, I commit myself to....

_____

_____

_____

_____

MAKE SPACE » What is on my mind, in my heart, or on my shoulders?

_____

_____

_____

_____

RELEASE » Let go of....

_____

_____

_____

_____

"We either make ourselves miserable or we make ourselves strong. The amount of work is the same."

- Carlos Castaneda

DATE: ___/___/_____

GRATITUDE » I am grateful for....
(write what you are grateful for and because)

1. _____
   _____

2. _____
   _____

3. _____
   _____

4. _____
   _____

5. _____
   _____

VISION » What would make today great?

_____

_____

_____

_____

_____

_____

Rise in Gratitude • Sheila Chasse

INTENTIONS » Today, I commit myself to....

_____

_____

_____

_____

MAKE SPACE » What is on my mind, in my heart, or on my shoulders?

_____

_____

_____

_____

RELEASE » Let go of....

_____

_____

_____

_____

"Gratitude is one of the sweet shortcuts to finding peace of mind and happiness inside. No matter what is going on outside of us, there is always something to be grateful for."

- Barry Neil Kaufman

DATE: ___/___/_____

GRATITUDE » I am grateful for....
(write what you are grateful for and because)

1. _____

_____

2. _____

_____

3. _____

_____

4. _____

_____

5. _____

_____

VISION » What would make today great?

_____

_____

_____

_____

_____

_____

INTENTIONS » Today, I commit myself to....

_____

_____

_____

_____

MAKE SPACE » What is on my mind, in my heart, or on my shoulders?

_____

_____

_____

_____

RELEASE » Let go of....

_____

_____

_____

_____

"The more grateful I am the more beauty I see."

- Mary Davis

DATE: ___/___/_____

GRATITUDE » I am grateful for....
(write what you are grateful for and because)

1. _____

   _____

2. _____

   _____

3. _____

   _____

4. _____

   _____

5. _____

   _____

VISION » What would make today great?

_____

_____

_____

_____

_____

_____

Rise in Gratitude • Sheila Chasse

INTENTIONS » Today, I commit myself to....

_____

_____

_____

_____

MAKE SPACE » What is on my mind, in my heart, or on my shoulders?

_____

_____

_____

_____

RELEASE » Let go of....

_____

_____

_____

_____

"It does not matter if the glass is half empty or half full.... Be grateful that you have a glass, and there is something in it."

- Unknown

DATE: ___/___/_____

GRATITUDE » I am grateful for....
(write what you are grateful for and because)

1. _____

   _____

2. _____

   _____

3. _____

   _____

4. _____

   _____

5. _____

   _____

VISION » What would make today great?

_____

_____

_____

_____

_____

_____

Rise in Gratitude • Sheila Chasse

INTENTIONS » Today, I commit myself to....

_____

_____

_____

_____

MAKE SPACE » What is on my mind, in my heart, or on my shoulders?

_____

_____

_____

_____

RELEASE » Let go of....

_____

_____

_____

_____

"Gratitude is one of the most medicinal emotions we can feel. It elevates our moods and fills us with joy."

- Sara Avant Stover

DATE: ___/___/_____

GRATITUDE » I am grateful for....
(write what you are grateful for and because)

1. _____

   _____

2. _____

   _____

3. _____

   _____

4. _____

   _____

5. _____

   _____

VISION » What would make today great?

_____

_____

_____

_____

_____

_____

Rise in Gratitude • Sheila Chasse

INTENTIONS » Today, I commit myself to....

_____

_____

_____

_____

MAKE SPACE » What is on my mind, in my heart, or on my shoulders?

_____

_____

_____

_____

RELEASE » Let go of....

_____

_____

_____

_____

"Gratitude is the vitamin for the soul."

- Unknown

GRATITUDE » I am grateful for....
(write what you are grateful for and because)

1. _____
   _____

2. _____
   _____

3. _____
   _____

4. _____
   _____

5. _____
   _____

VISION » What would make today great?

_____

_____

_____

_____

_____

_____

INTENTIONS » Today, I commit myself to....

_____

_____

_____

_____

MAKE SPACE » What is on my mind, in my heart, or on my shoulders?

_____

_____

_____

_____

RELEASE » Let go of....

_____

_____

_____

_____

"Being grateful all the time is not easy. But it is when you least feel thankful that you are most in need of what gratitude can give you: perspective. Gratitude can transform any situation. It alters your vibration, moving you from negative energy to positive. It is the quickest, easiest most powerful way to effect change in your life – this I know for sure."

- Oprah Winfrey

Give
YOURSELF A GIFT

A DOSE OF INSPIRATION

Give yourself a gift today and I am not talking about something tangible, but something much deeper than that. I want you to go the entire day without saying any negative self-judgements to yourself. Sometimes we do not even notice the voice or record playing over and over in our heads that can fuel us the wrong way so watch closely and release all negative statements made about yourself and replace them with something good and positive. Do this as an experiment to find out what this feels like. You might be absolutely amazed at the transformation in your experience.

Being critical of yourself and speaking negatively of yourself has never worked to propel you further so try approving of yourself and having a grateful mindset of just having the simple opportunity for a new day, a new chance to go after what you want, and so forth and watch what happens.

HERE IS TO A NEW WEEK AHEAD! EACH WEEK WE START OFF WITH THIS!

The life you want is on the other side of that "stuff" you do not want to do. You have a whole new week ahead of you and though we cannot know what will be in store for us, we can start with a grateful heart and utilize the time we so graciously have been given. With that being said, use the space below to jot down what you aim to accomplish or tackle in the week to come. Do not overwhelm yourself with a huge To-Do List as too much listed is not a good thing. Keep it short and attainable, setting realistic goals.

List 3 things that would help you feel a sense of clarity and accomplishment if you completed them this week.

Make it a practical list of attainable goals so you can check off small wins this week. Instead of an overwhelming project like, "Clean out the garage" try, "Put kids' summer toys in big gray bin and store under the stairs." Remember, it's "progress, not perfection."

To Do's

1.

2.

3.

DATE: ___/___/_____

GRATITUDE » I am grateful for....
(write what you are grateful for and because)

1. _____

   _____

2. _____

   _____

3. _____

   _____

4. _____

   _____

5. _____

   _____

VISION » What would make today great?

_____

_____

_____

_____

_____

_____

Rise in Gratitude • Sheila Chasse

INTENTIONS » Today, I commit myself to....

_____

_____

_____

_____

MAKE SPACE » What is on my mind, in my heart, or on my shoulders?

_____

_____

_____

_____

RELEASE » Let go of....

_____

_____

_____

_____

"Gratitude RX: Take a dose every morning. May cause shifts in perspective. May cause feelings of abundance. Decreased feelings of fear and anxiety."

- Unknown

DATE: ___/___/_____

GRATITUDE » I am grateful for....
(write what you are grateful for and because)

1. _____

   _____

2. _____

   _____

3. _____

   _____

4. _____

   _____

5. _____

   _____

VISION » What would make today great?

_____

_____

_____

_____

_____

_____

INTENTIONS » Today, I commit myself to....

_____

_____

_____

_____

MAKE SPACE » What is on my mind, in my heart, or on my shoulders?

_____

_____

_____

_____

RELEASE » Let go of....

_____

_____

_____

_____

"Gratitude unlocks the fullness of life. It turns problems into gifts, failures into success, the unexpected into perfect timing, and mistakes into important events. Gratitude makes sense of our past, brings peace for today and creates a vision for tomorrow."

- Melody Beattie

DATE: ___/___/_____

GRATITUDE » I am grateful for....
(write what you are grateful for and because)

1. _____

_____

2. _____

_____

3. _____

_____

4. _____

_____

5. _____

_____

VISION » What would make today great?

_____

_____

_____

_____

_____

_____

Rise in Gratitude • Sheila Chasse

INTENTIONS » Today, I commit myself to....

_____

_____

_____

_____

MAKE SPACE » What is on my mind, in my heart, or on my shoulders?

_____

_____

_____

_____

RELEASE » Let go of....

_____

_____

_____

_____

"Gratitude is acknowledging the goodness in our lives as life exists today, not as we wish it to be."

- Unknown

DATE: ___/___/_____

GRATITUDE » I am grateful for....
(write what you are grateful for and because)

1. _____

_____

2. _____

_____

3. _____

_____

4. _____

_____

5. _____

_____

VISION » What would make today great?

_____

_____

_____

_____

_____

_____

Rise in Gratitude • Sheila Chasse

INTENTIONS » Today, I commit myself to....

_____

_____

_____

_____

MAKE SPACE » What is on my mind, in my heart, or on my shoulders?

_____

_____

_____

_____

RELEASE » Let go of....

_____

_____

_____

_____

"We have to fill our hearts with gratitude. Gratitude makes everything that we have more than enough."

- Susan L. Taylor

DATE: ___/___/_____

GRATITUDE » I am grateful for....
(write what you are grateful for and because)

1. _____
   _____

2. _____
   _____

3. _____
   _____

4. _____
   _____

5. _____
   _____

VISION » What would make today great?

_____

_____

_____

_____

_____

_____

Rise in Gratitude • Sheila Chasse

INTENTIONS » Today, I commit myself to....

_____

_____

_____

_____

MAKE SPACE » What is on my mind, in my heart, or on my shoulders?

_____

_____

_____

_____

RELEASE » Let go of....

_____

_____

_____

_____

"Gratitude is the healthiest of all human emotions."

- Zig Ziglar

DATE: ___/___/_____

GRATITUDE » I am grateful for....
(write what you are grateful for and because)

1. _____
   _____

2. _____
   _____

3. _____
   _____

4. _____
   _____

5. _____
   _____

VISION » What would make today great?

_____

_____

_____

_____

_____

_____

Rise in Gratitude • Sheila Chasse

INTENTIONS » Today, I commit myself to....

_____

_____

_____

_____

MAKE SPACE » What is on my mind, in my heart, or on my shoulders?

_____

_____

_____

_____

RELEASE » Let go of....

_____

_____

_____

_____

"We can only be said to be alive in those moments when our hearts are conscious of our treasures."

- Thornton Wilder

DATE: ___/___/_____

GRATITUDE » I am grateful for....
(write what you are grateful for and because)

1. _____

   _____

2. _____

   _____

3. _____

   _____

4. _____

   _____

5. _____

   _____

VISION » What would make today great?

_____

_____

_____

_____

_____

_____

INTENTIONS » Today, I commit myself to....

_____

_____

_____

_____

MAKE SPACE » What is on my mind, in my heart, or on my shoulders?

_____

_____

_____

_____

RELEASE » Let go of....

_____

_____

_____

_____

"Gratitude breathes life into the soul."

- Unknown

I AM

I am powerful beyond measure,

Stronger than I think,

Braver than I seem,

Blessed with all I need.

I am here to love;

I am here to serve;

I am here to uplift,

To grow and give;

I am born to thrive;

I am glad to be alive;

I claim my right,

To live a great life.

- Author Unknown

HERE IS TO A NEW WEEK AHEAD! EACH WEEK WE START OFF WITH THIS!

The life you want is on the other side of that "stuff" you do not want to do. You have a whole new week ahead of you and though we cannot know what will be in store for us, we can start with a grateful heart and utilize the time we so graciously have been given. With that being said, use the space below to jot down what you aim to accomplish or tackle in the week to come. Do not overwhelm yourself with a huge To-Do List as too much listed is not a good thing. Keep it short and attainable, setting realistic goals.

List 3 things that would help you feel a sense of clarity and accomplishment if you completed them this week.

Make it a practical list of attainable goals so you can check off small wins this week. Instead of an overwhelming project like, "Clean out the garage" try, "Put kids' summer toys in big gray bin and store under the stairs." Remember, it's "progress, not perfection."

To Do's

1.

2.

3.

DATE: ___/___/_____

GRATITUDE » I am grateful for....
(write what you are grateful for and because)

1. _____

   _____

2. _____

   _____

3. _____

   _____

4. _____

   _____

5. _____

   _____

VISION » What would make today great?

_____

_____

_____

_____

_____

_____

Rise in Gratitude • Sheila Chasse

INTENTIONS » Today, I commit myself to....

_____

_____

_____

_____

MAKE SPACE » What is on my mind, in my heart, or on my shoulders?

_____

_____

_____

_____

RELEASE » Let go of....

_____

_____

_____

_____

"Spend the day appreciating every little thing that comes your way, and you will end the day feeling deeply grateful for your life."

- Grateful Soul

DATE: ___/___/_____

GRATITUDE » I am grateful for....
(write what you are grateful for and because)

1. _____

   _____

2. _____

   _____

3. _____

   _____

4. _____

   _____

5. _____

   _____

VISION » What would make today great?

_____

_____

_____

_____

_____

_____

INTENTIONS » Today, I commit myself to....

_____

_____

_____

_____

MAKE SPACE » What is on my mind, in my heart, or on my shoulders?

_____

_____

_____

_____

RELEASE » Let go of....

_____

_____

_____

_____

"God gave you a gift of 84,600 seconds today. Have you used one of them to say Thank You?"

- William Arthur Ward

DATE: ___/___/_____

GRATITUDE » I am grateful for....
(write what you are grateful for and because)

1. _____
   _____

2. _____
   _____

3. _____
   _____

4. _____
   _____

5. _____
   _____

VISION » What would make today great?

_____

_____

_____

_____

_____

_____

Rise in Gratitude • Sheila Chasse

INTENTIONS » Today, I commit myself to....

_____

_____

_____

_____

MAKE SPACE » What is on my mind, in my heart, or on my shoulders?

_____

_____

_____

_____

RELEASE » Let go of....

_____

_____

_____

_____

"Keep your soul rooted in gratitude and
your branches open to blessings."

- Mary Davis

DATE: ___/___/_____

GRATITUDE » I am grateful for....
(write what you are grateful for and because)

1. _____
   _____

2. _____
   _____

3. _____
   _____

4. _____
   _____

5. _____
   _____

VISION » What would make today great?

_____

_____

_____

_____

_____

_____

Rise in Gratitude • Sheila Chasse

INTENTIONS » Today, I commit myself to....

_____

_____

_____

_____

MAKE SPACE » What is on my mind, in my heart, or on my shoulders?

_____

_____

_____

_____

RELEASE » Let go of....

_____

_____

_____

_____

"Gratitude is an antidote to negative emotions, a neutralizer of envy, hostility, worry, and irritation. It is savoring; it is not taking things for granted; it is present oriented."

- Sonja Lyubomirsky

DATE: ___/___/_____

GRATITUDE » I am grateful for....
(write what you are grateful for and because)

1. _____
   _____

2. _____
   _____

3. _____
   _____

4. _____
   _____

5. _____
   _____

VISION » What would make today great?

_____

_____

_____

_____

_____

_____

Rise in Gratitude • Sheila Chasse

INTENTIONS » Today, I commit myself to....

_____

_____

_____

_____

MAKE SPACE » What is on my mind, in my heart, or on my shoulders?

_____

_____

_____

_____

RELEASE » Let go of....

_____

_____

_____

_____

"A grateful mind is a great mind which eventually attracts to itself great things."

- Plato

DATE: ___/___/_____

GRATITUDE » I am grateful for….
(write what you are grateful for and because)

1. _____

_____

2. _____

_____

3. _____

_____

4. _____

_____

5. _____

_____

VISION » What would make today great?

_____

_____

_____

_____

_____

_____

Rise in Gratitude • Sheila Chasse

INTENTIONS » Today, I commit myself to....

_____

_____

_____

_____

MAKE SPACE » What is on my mind, in my heart, or on my shoulders?

_____

_____

_____

_____

RELEASE » Let go of....

_____

_____

_____

_____

"Sometimes we should express our gratitude for the small and simple things like the scent of rain, the taste of your favorite food, or the sound of a loved one's voice."

- Joseph B. Wirthlin

DATE: ___/___/_____

GRATITUDE » I am grateful for….
(write what you are grateful for and because)

1. _____

   _____

2. _____

   _____

3. _____

   _____

4. _____

   _____

5. _____

   _____

VISION » What would make today great?

_____

_____

_____

_____

_____

_____

INTENTIONS » Today, I commit myself to....

_____

_____

_____

_____

MAKE SPACE » What is on my mind, in my heart, or on my shoulders?

_____

_____

_____

_____

RELEASE » Let go of....

_____

_____

_____

_____

"I manifest abundance by being grateful for what I already have."

- Unknown

Purpose

There is nothing more powerful than someone with PURPOSE. When you know what your WHY is, why you are fighting, why you choose to get up each morning and dedicate time to yourself to fuel yourself (like gratitude for an example), why you are pushing onward, why you are not giving in or up, then you know and have a PURPOSE. You will outwork anyone and everyone with that kind of drive. That purpose driven kind of drive. Not just the "hustle" we hear so many saying... no, with purpose it goes MUCH deeper than the hustle. With purpose behind you, you will give more, do more, and become more. You will not give up when things go against you because at times they will. You will fight on for your goals, your dreams, and your WHY. Then and only then your weaknesses will no longer limit you and those weaknesses can become teachers. They can show us what we need to work on or let go of while remaining in a state of gratitude either way.

And know that there will always be people who will have more talent than you, they may be bigger than you, stronger than you, but they will never out work the purpose driven person you are! You can never out push, out courage, or out heart someone who fights and continues through life with purpose and a grateful heart.

HERE IS TO A NEW WEEK AHEAD! EACH WEEK WE START OFF WITH THIS!

The life you want is on the other side of that "stuff" you do not want to do. You have a whole new week ahead of you and though we cannot know what will be in store for us, we can start with a grateful heart and utilize the time we so graciously have been given. With that being said, use the space below to jot down what you aim to accomplish or tackle in the week to come. Do not overwhelm yourself with a huge To-Do List as too much listed is not a good thing. Keep it short and attainable, setting realistic goals.

List 3 things that would help you feel a sense of clarity and accomplishment if you completed them this week.

Make it a practical list of attainable goals so you can check off small wins this week. Instead of an overwhelming project like, "Clean out the garage" try, "Put kids' summer toys in big gray bin and store under the stairs." Remember, it's "progress, not perfection."

To Do's

1.

2.

3.

DATE: ___/___/_____

GRATITUDE » I am grateful for....
(write what you are grateful for and because)

1. _____

   _____

2. _____

   _____

3. _____

   _____

4. _____

   _____

5. _____

   _____

VISION » What would make today great?

_____

_____

_____

_____

_____

_____

Rise in Gratitude • Sheila Chasse

INTENTIONS » Today, I commit myself to....

_____

_____

_____

_____

MAKE SPACE » What is on my mind, in my heart, or on my shoulders?

_____

_____

_____

_____

RELEASE » Let go of....

_____

_____

_____

_____

"True self-care is not bath salts and chocolate cake, it is making the choice to build a life you do not need to escape from."

- Brianna Wiest

DATE: ___/___/_____

GRATITUDE » I am grateful for....
(write what you are grateful for and because)

1. _____
   _____

2. _____
   _____

3. _____
   _____

4. _____
   _____

5. _____
   _____

VISION » What would make today great?

_____

_____

_____

_____

_____

_____

INTENTIONS » Today, I commit myself to....

_____

_____

_____

_____

MAKE SPACE » What is on my mind, in my heart, or on my shoulders?

_____

_____

_____

_____

RELEASE » Let go of....

_____

_____

_____

_____

"By feeling and practicing gratitude in your waking day, you are in a state to receive. You are in an energy that is drawing something to you on a moment-to-moment basis."

- Dr. Joe Dispenza

DATE: ___/___/_____

GRATITUDE » I am grateful for....
(write what you are grateful for and because)

1. _____

   _____

2. _____

   _____

3. _____

   _____

4. _____

   _____

5. _____

   _____

VISION » What would make today great?

_____

_____

_____

_____

_____

_____

Rise in Gratitude • Sheila Chasse

INTENTIONS » Today, I commit myself to....

_____

_____

_____

_____

MAKE SPACE » What is on my mind, in my heart, or on my shoulders?

_____

_____

_____

_____

RELEASE » Let go of....

_____

_____

_____

_____

"When you are grateful, an invisible blanket of peace covers you, it makes you glow, it makes you happy, strong, warm. Gratitude puts the mind at ease about everything around."

- Om Swami

DATE: ___/___/_____

GRATITUDE » I am grateful for....
(write what you are grateful for and because)

1. _____
   _____

2. _____
   _____

3. _____
   _____

4. _____
   _____

5. _____
   _____

VISION » What would make today great?

_____
_____
_____
_____
_____
_____

Rise in Gratitude • Sheila Chasse

INTENTIONS » Today, I commit myself to....

_____

_____

_____

_____

MAKE SPACE » What is on my mind, in my heart, or on my shoulders?

_____

_____

_____

_____

RELEASE » Let go of....

_____

_____

_____

_____

"Be thankful for what you have; you will end up having more. If you concentrate on what you do not have, you will never, ever have enough."

- Oprah Winfrey

DATE: ___/___/_____

GRATITUDE » I am grateful for....
(write what you are grateful for and because)

1. _____

   _____

2. _____

   _____

3. _____

   _____

4. _____

   _____

5. _____

   _____

VISION » What would make today great?

_____

_____

_____

_____

_____

_____

INTENTIONS » Today, I commit myself to....

_____

_____

_____

_____

MAKE SPACE » What is on my mind, in my heart, or on my shoulders?

_____

_____

_____

_____

RELEASE » Let go of....

_____

_____

_____

_____

"We all have a bag. We all pack differently. Some of us are traveling light. Some of us are secret hoarders who have never parted with a memory in our lives. I think we are all called to figure out how to carry our bag to the best of our ability, how to unpack it, and how to face the mess. I think part of growing up is learning how to sit down on the floor with all your things and figure out what to take with you and what to leave behind."

- Hannah Brencher

DATE: ___/___/_____

GRATITUDE » I am grateful for....
(write what you are grateful for and because)

1. _____

_____

2. _____

_____

3. _____

_____

4. _____

_____

5. _____

_____

VISION » What would make today great?

_____

_____

_____

_____

_____

_____

Rise in Gratitude • Sheila Chasse

INTENTIONS » Today, I commit myself to....

_____

_____

_____

_____

MAKE SPACE » What is on my mind, in my heart, or on my shoulders?

_____

_____

_____

_____

RELEASE » Let go of....

_____

_____

_____

_____

"Gratitude enables our hearts to tell a better story."

- Unknown

DATE: ___/___/_____

GRATITUDE » I am grateful for....
(write what you are grateful for and because)

1. _____
   _____

2. _____
   _____

3. _____
   _____

4. _____
   _____

5. _____
   _____

VISION » What would make today great?

_____
_____
_____
_____
_____
_____

Rise in Gratitude • Sheila Chasse

INTENTIONS » Today, I commit myself to....

_____

_____

_____

_____

MAKE SPACE » What is on my mind, in my heart, or on my shoulders?

_____

_____

_____

_____

RELEASE » Let go of....

_____

_____

_____

_____

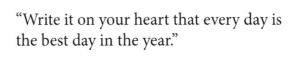

"Write it on your heart that every day is
the best day in the year."

- Ralph Waldo Emerson

DO EVERYTHING WITH A

Joyful Heart

No matter what is going on in your world, no matter what happens today—do everything with a joyful heart, even when it is not easy. During the highs and lows, choose a stance of celebration.

"Every day, choose to find something to be thankful for, decide to find the gold, and resolve to look for the happy moments. If you cannot find anything to be joyful about, remember this: you are alive with a beating heart and air flowing through your lungs. This means your work here is not finished, and you have not reached your story's end. You continue to have a purpose; you have a dream that needs you to bring it to LIFE. That is something to be joyful about and celebrate."

– Unknown

HERE IS TO A NEW WEEK AHEAD! EACH WEEK WE START OFF WITH THIS!

The life you want is on the other side of that "stuff" you do not want to do. You have a whole new week ahead of you and though we cannot know what will be in store for us, we can start with a grateful heart and utilize the time we so graciously have been given. With that being said, use the space below to jot down what you aim to accomplish or tackle in the week to come. Do not overwhelm yourself with a huge To-Do List as too much listed is not a good thing. Keep it short and attainable, setting realistic goals.

List 3 things that would help you feel a sense of clarity and accomplishment if you completed them this week.

Make it a practical list of attainable goals so you can check off small wins this week. Instead of an overwhelming project like, "Clean out the garage" try, "Put kids' summer toys in big gray bin and store under the stairs." Remember, it's "progress, not perfection."

To Do's

1.

2.

3.

DATE: ___/___/_____

GRATITUDE » I am grateful for....
(write what you are grateful for and because)

1. _____
   _____

2. _____
   _____

3. _____
   _____

4. _____
   _____

5. _____
   _____

VISION » What would make today great?

_____

_____

_____

_____

_____

_____

Rise in Gratitude • Sheila Chasse

INTENTIONS » Today, I commit myself to....

_____

_____

_____

_____

MAKE SPACE » What is on my mind, in my heart, or on my shoulders?

_____

_____

_____

_____

RELEASE » Let go of....

_____

_____

_____

_____

"The idea of "success," for most people, revolves around money or the acquisition of property or other possessions, but we consider a state of joy as the greatest achievement of success. And while the attainment of money and wonderful possessions certainly can enhance your state of joy, the achievement of the good-feeling physical body is by far the greatest factor for maintaining a continuing state of joy and well-being. And so, there are few things of greater value than the achievement of a good-feeling body."

- Abraham-Hicks

DATE: ___/___/_____

GRATITUDE » I am grateful for....
(write what you are grateful for and because)

1. _____
   _____

2. _____
   _____

3. _____
   _____

4. _____
   _____

5. _____
   _____

VISION » What would make today great?

_____
_____
_____
_____
_____
_____

Rise in Gratitude • Sheila Chasse

INTENTIONS » Today, I commit myself to....

_____

_____

_____

_____

MAKE SPACE » What is on my mind, in my heart, or on my shoulders?

_____

_____

_____

_____

RELEASE » Let go of....

_____

_____

_____

_____

"Gratitude can turn a meal into a feast, a house into a home, and a stranger into a friend."

- Melody Beattie

DATE: ___/___/_____

GRATITUDE » I am grateful for....
(write what you are grateful for and because)

1. _____

_____

2. _____

_____

3. _____

_____

4. _____

_____

5. _____

_____

VISION » What would make today great?

_____

_____

_____

_____

_____

_____

Rise in Gratitude • Sheila Chasse

INTENTIONS » Today, I commit myself to....

_____

_____

_____

_____

MAKE SPACE » What is on my mind, in my heart, or on my shoulders?

_____

_____

_____

_____

RELEASE » Let go of....

_____

_____

_____

_____

"Gratitude helps you to grow and expand; gratitude brings joy and laughter into your life and into the lives of all those around you."

- Eileen Caddy

DATE: ___/___/_____

GRATITUDE » I am grateful for....
(write what you are grateful for and because)

1. _____
   _____

2. _____
   _____

3. _____
   _____

4. _____
   _____

5. _____
   _____

VISION » What would make today great?

_____

_____

_____

_____

_____

_____

Rise in Gratitude • Sheila Chasse

INTENTIONS » Today, I commit myself to....

_____

_____

_____

_____

MAKE SPACE » What is on my mind, in my heart, or on my shoulders?

_____

_____

_____

_____

RELEASE » Let go of....

_____

_____

_____

_____

"Inhale Love. Exhale Gratitude."

- Unknown

DATE: ___ / ___ / _____

GRATITUDE » I am grateful for....
(write what you are grateful for and because)

1. _____

   _____

2. _____

   _____

3. _____

   _____

4. _____

   _____

5. _____

   _____

VISION » What would make today great?

_____

_____

_____

_____

_____

_____

INTENTIONS » Today, I commit myself to....

_____

_____

_____

_____

MAKE SPACE » What is on my mind, in my heart, or on my shoulders?

_____

_____

_____

_____

RELEASE » Let go of....

_____

_____

_____

_____

"If you must look back, do so forgivingly. If you must look forward, do so prayerfully. However, the wisest thing you can do is be present in the present... gratefully."

- Maya Angelou

DATE: ___/___/_____

GRATITUDE » I am grateful for....
(write what you are grateful for and because)

1. _____
   _____

2. _____
   _____

3. _____
   _____

4. _____
   _____

5. _____
   _____

VISION » What would make today great?

_____

_____

_____

_____

_____

_____

Rise in Gratitude • Sheila Chasse

INTENTIONS » Today, I commit myself to….

_____

_____

_____

_____

MAKE SPACE » What is on my mind, in my heart, or on my shoulders?

_____

_____

_____

_____

RELEASE » Let go of….

_____

_____

_____

_____

"Some people could be given an entire field of roses and only see the thorns in it. Others could be given a single weed and only see the wildflower in it. Perception is a key component to gratitude. And gratitude a key component to joy."

- Amy Weatherly

DATE: ___/___/_____

GRATITUDE » I am grateful for....
(write what you are grateful for and because)

1. _____
   _____

2. _____
   _____

3. _____
   _____

4. _____
   _____

5. _____
   _____

VISION » What would make today great?

_____

_____

_____

_____

_____

_____

Rise in Gratitude • Sheila Chasse

INTENTIONS » Today, I commit myself to….

_____

_____

_____

_____

MAKE SPACE » What is on my mind, in my heart, or on my shoulders?

_____

_____

_____

_____

RELEASE » Let go of….

_____

_____

_____

_____

"Gratitude is a magnifying glass. When you are grateful for the little things, they become the big things that fuel you with so much joy and meaning."

- Nataly Kogan

DO NOT LET WORRY

Rob You

We do not know what tomorrow will bring so let tomorrow worry about itself. Most of us have heard this saying in some form, but it really is so important to apply intentional to our worrying thoughts that can take over. Worrying only takes away our current peace. Try letting worry be a passing moment, notice it and do not judge it, then let it go. Do not let it be the compass for your life. It will lead to nowhere, only lost time. Instead, try using how you would like to feel to guide you forward. Even amongst the uncomfortable worry you may feel, imagine how you would rather be feeling and that can be a catalyst for creating positive change amongst the worry.

Just know, as we all need the reminder sometimes, that worrying will not stop tough things from happening. It just stops you from enjoying the good that is happening and keeps you from being present in the moment of all that is around you, and all that you have to be grateful for. Let gratitude help you combat your worry.

HERE IS TO A NEW WEEK AHEAD! EACH WEEK WE START OFF WITH THIS!

The life you want is on the other side of that "stuff" you do not want to do. You have a whole new week ahead of you and though we cannot know what will be in store for us, we can start with a grateful heart and utilize the time we so graciously have been given. With that being said, use the space below to jot down what you aim to accomplish or tackle in the week to come. Do not overwhelm yourself with a huge To-Do List as too much listed is not a good thing. Keep it short and attainable, setting realistic goals.

List 3 things that would help you feel a sense of clarity and accomplishment if you completed them this week.

Make it a practical list of attainable goals so you can check off small wins this week. Instead of an overwhelming project like, "Clean out the garage" try, "Put kids' summer toys in big gray bin and store under the stairs." Remember, it's "progress, not perfection."

To Do's

1.

2.

3.

DATE: ___/___/_____

GRATITUDE » I am grateful for....
(write what you are grateful for and because)

1. _____

_____

2. _____

_____

3. _____

_____

4. _____

_____

5. _____

_____

VISION » What would make today great?

_____

_____

_____

_____

_____

_____

Rise in Gratitude • Sheila Chasse

INTENTIONS » Today, I commit myself to....

_____

_____

_____

_____

MAKE SPACE » What is on my mind, in my heart, or on my shoulders?

_____

_____

_____

_____

RELEASE » Let go of....

_____

_____

_____

_____

"Things to be grateful for: What left. What stayed. And what is on the way."

- Nakeia Homer

DATE: ___/___/_____

GRATITUDE » I am grateful for....
(write what you are grateful for and because)

1. _____
   _____

2. _____
   _____

3. _____
   _____

4. _____
   _____

5. _____
   _____

VISION » What would make today great?

_____

_____

_____

_____

_____

_____

Rise in Gratitude • Sheila Chasse

INTENTIONS » Today, I commit myself to....

_____

_____

_____

_____

MAKE SPACE » What is on my mind, in my heart, or on my shoulders?

_____

_____

_____

_____

RELEASE » Let go of....

_____

_____

_____

_____

"Don't let your dreams blind you from your blessings."

- Unknown

DATE: ___/___/_____

GRATITUDE » I am grateful for....
(write what you are grateful for and because)

1. _____

_____

2. _____

_____

3. _____

_____

4. _____

_____

5. _____

_____

VISION » What would make today great?

_____

_____

_____

_____

_____

_____

INTENTIONS » Today, I commit myself to....

_____

_____

_____

_____

MAKE SPACE » What is on my mind, in my heart, or on my shoulders?

_____

_____

_____

_____

RELEASE » Let go of....

_____

_____

_____

_____

"Frustration cannot thrive in a mind set on rejoicing."

- Unknown

DATE: ___/___/_____

GRATITUDE » I am grateful for....
(write what you are grateful for and because)

1. _____
_____

2. _____
_____

3. _____
_____

4. _____
_____

5. _____
_____

VISION » What would make today great?

_____

_____

_____

_____

_____

_____

INTENTIONS » Today, I commit myself to....

_____

_____

_____

_____

MAKE SPACE » What is on my mind, in my heart, or on my shoulders?

_____

_____

_____

_____

RELEASE » Let go of....

_____

_____

_____

_____

"Wear gratitude like a cloak and it will feed every corner of your life."

- Rumi

DATE: ___/___/_____

GRATITUDE » I am grateful for....
(write what you are grateful for and because)

1. _____
   _____

2. _____
   _____

3. _____
   _____

4. _____
   _____

5. _____
   _____

VISION » What would make today great?

_____
_____
_____
_____
_____
_____

Rise in Gratitude • Sheila Chasse

INTENTIONS » Today, I commit myself to....

_____

_____

_____

_____

MAKE SPACE » What is on my mind, in my heart, or on my shoulders?

_____

_____

_____

_____

RELEASE » Let go of....

_____

_____

_____

_____

"Gratitude is our most direct line to God and the angels. The more we seek gratitude the more reason the angels will give us for gratitude and joy to exist in our lives."

- Unknown

DATE: ___/___/_____

GRATITUDE » I am grateful for....
(write what you are grateful for and because)

1. _____
   _____

2. _____
   _____

3. _____
   _____

4. _____
   _____

5. _____
   _____

VISION » What would make today great?

_____

_____

_____

_____

_____

_____

Rise in Gratitude • Sheila Chasse

INTENTIONS » Today, I commit myself to....

_____

_____

_____

_____

MAKE SPACE » What is on my mind, in my heart, or on my shoulders?

_____

_____

_____

_____

RELEASE » Let go of....

_____

_____

_____

_____

"Gratitude inspires happiness and carries divine influence."

- Bonnie D. Parkin

DATE: ___/___/_____

GRATITUDE » I am grateful for....
(write what you are grateful for and because)

1. _____

   _____

2. _____

   _____

3. _____

   _____

4. _____

   _____

5. _____

   _____

VISION » What would make today great?

_____

_____

_____

_____

_____

_____

Rise in Gratitude • Sheila Chasse

INTENTIONS » Today, I commit myself to....

_____

_____

_____

_____

MAKE SPACE » What is on my mind, in my heart, or on my shoulders?

_____

_____

_____

_____

RELEASE » Let go of....

_____

_____

_____

_____

"Approach today with gratitude, understanding, openness; knowing that it offers potential and possibilities. Knowing that every moment is an opportunity to reflect, reset, and move forward with intention."

- Unknown

THE MIND IS

Everything

As you have read in this book and come to understand through this practice of gratitude, your mind is a powerful thing. A quote that I love which sums this up is, "What you think, you become. What you feel, you attract. What you imagine, you create." -Buddha

This is so true with the practice of gratitude. Just think, what if you woke up tomorrow and were only surrounded by the things you felt gratitude for daily? What would that look like for you?

And what if you woke up tomorrow and were only surrounded by the things that you complained about?

It kind of works that way! The vibration of gratitude is intense and when you intentionally focus on gratitude and all that you have to be grateful for while pushing aside the complaining, it attracts more positive things into your life. I am not saying that things will always be butterflies and rainbows just by implementing gratitude, but gratitude will help you see things in a whole new light, and it will help transform how you react and hang on to things such as anger, sadness, resentment, and so much more. It will not matter if the glass is half empty or half full so to say, but what will matter is that you have a glass to use in the first dang place!

Here is the big takeaway. Do not try to calm the storm you might be currently going through. Calm your MIND first. Use your gratitude practices or whatever else it is that you use to calm your mind and watch how the storm will pass without draining you dry and without stealing your inner peace.

HERE IS TO A NEW WEEK AHEAD! EACH WEEK WE START OFF WITH THIS!

The life you want is on the other side of that "stuff" you do not want to do. You have a whole new week ahead of you and though we cannot know what will be in store for us, we can start with a grateful heart and utilize the time we so graciously have been given. With that being said, use the space below to jot down what you aim to accomplish or tackle in the week to come. Do not overwhelm yourself with a huge To-Do List as too much listed is not a good thing. Keep it short and attainable, setting realistic goals.

List 3 things that would help you feel a sense of clarity and accomplishment if you completed them this week.

Make it a practical list of attainable goals so you can check off small wins this week. Instead of an overwhelming project like, "Clean out the garage" try, "Put kids' summer toys in big gray bin and store under the stairs." Remember, it's "progress, not perfection."

To Do's

1.

2.

3.

DATE: ___/___/_____

GRATITUDE » I am grateful for....
(write what you are grateful for and because)

1. _____
   _____

2. _____
   _____

3. _____
   _____

4. _____
   _____

5. _____
   _____

VISION » What would make today great?

_____

_____

_____

_____

_____

_____

Rise in Gratitude • Sheila Chasse

INTENTIONS » Today, I commit myself to....

_____

_____

_____

_____

MAKE SPACE » What is on my mind, in my heart, or on my shoulders?

_____

_____

_____

_____

RELEASE » Let go of....

_____

_____

_____

_____

"Gratitude and attitude are not challenges;
they are choices."

- Robert Braathe

DATE: ___/___/_____

GRATITUDE » I am grateful for....
(write what you are grateful for and because)

1. _____
   _____

2. _____
   _____

3. _____
   _____

4. _____
   _____

5. _____
   _____

VISION » What would make today great?

_____
_____
_____
_____
_____
_____

Rise in Gratitude • Sheila Chasse

INTENTIONS » Today, I commit myself to....

_____

_____

_____

_____

MAKE SPACE » What is on my mind, in my heart, or on my shoulders?

_____

_____

_____

_____

RELEASE » Let go of....

_____

_____

_____

_____

"The moment you start acting like life is a blessing, it starts feeling like one."

- Unknown

DATE: ___/___/_____

GRATITUDE » I am grateful for....
(write what you are grateful for and because)

1. _____
   _____

2. _____
   _____

3. _____
   _____

4. _____
   _____

5. _____
   _____

VISION » What would make today great?

_____
_____
_____
_____
_____
_____

Rise in Gratitude • Sheila Chasse

INTENTIONS » Today, I commit myself to....

_____

_____

_____

_____

MAKE SPACE » What is on my mind, in my heart, or on my shoulders?

_____

_____

_____

_____

RELEASE » Let go of....

_____

_____

_____

_____

"When you arise in the morning give thanks for the food and the joy of living. If you see no reason for giving thanks, the fault lies only in yourself."

- Tecumseh

DATE: ___/___/_____

GRATITUDE » I am grateful for....
(write what you are grateful for and because)

1. _____

   _____

2. _____

   _____

3. _____

   _____

4. _____

   _____

5. _____

   _____

VISION » What would make today great?

_____

_____

_____

_____

_____

_____

Rise in Gratitude • Sheila Chasse

INTENTIONS » Today, I commit myself to....

_____

_____

_____

_____

MAKE SPACE » What is on my mind, in my heart, or on my shoulders?

_____

_____

_____

_____

RELEASE » Let go of....

_____

_____

_____

_____

"Somebody did not wake up today, but you did. That is enough reason to stop complaining, and that is enough to be thankful for. Never let your troubles blind you to your daily blessings."

- Trent Shelton

DATE: ___/___/_____

GRATITUDE » I am grateful for....
(write what you are grateful for and because)

1. _____
   _____

2. _____
   _____

3. _____
   _____

4. _____
   _____

5. _____
   _____

VISION » What would make today great?

_____

_____

_____

_____

_____

_____

Rise in Gratitude • Sheila Chasse

INTENTIONS » Today, I commit myself to....

_____

_____

_____

_____

MAKE SPACE » What is on my mind, in my heart, or on my shoulders?

_____

_____

_____

_____

RELEASE » Let go of....

_____

_____

_____

_____

"Gratitude brings warmth to the giver and the receiver alike."

- Robert D. Hales

DATE: ___/___/_____

GRATITUDE » I am grateful for....
(write what you are grateful for and because)

1. _____

   _____

2. _____

   _____

3. _____

   _____

4. _____

   _____

5. _____

   _____

VISION » What would make today great?

_____

_____

_____

_____

_____

_____

Rise in Gratitude • Sheila Chasse

INTENTIONS » Today, I commit myself to....

_____

_____

_____

_____

MAKE SPACE » What is on my mind, in my heart, or on my shoulders?

_____

_____

_____

_____

RELEASE » Let go of....

_____

_____

_____

_____

"Don't pray when it rains if you don't pray when the sun shines."

- Unknown

DATE: ___/___/_____

GRATITUDE » I am grateful for....
(write what you are grateful for and because)

1. _____

   _____

2. _____

   _____

3. _____

   _____

4. _____

   _____

5. _____

   _____

VISION » What would make today great?

_____

_____

_____

_____

_____

_____

Rise in Gratitude • Sheila Chasse

INTENTIONS » Today, I commit myself to....

_____

_____

_____

_____

MAKE SPACE » What is on my mind, in my heart, or on my shoulders?

_____

_____

_____

_____

RELEASE » Let go of....

_____

_____

_____

_____

"I am grateful for the chances that life offers me each day to start over and create the life that I want. I am grateful for the fact that I can learn from my mistakes, and then let them go. I am grateful that the universe supports me with unconditional love, to be the happiest, best person that I can be."

- Saratoga Ocean

MAKE A

Commitment

I love this practice I came across from the book called, "The Secret," by Rhonda Byrne. Starting today, make the commitment for the next week or next month, whichever you think you can dedicate to, to give thanks each day. Every day during this committed time look for things to be grateful for. Make "thank you" your catchphrase. As you walk from one place to another, say "thank you," and let your last thought at night be one of giving thanks for the day you had. Be grateful under ALL circumstances, no matter what is happening around you. Just a week or a month (whichever you choose to do) of saturating yourself with gratitude, beyond just your journal entries. It will continue to change your life beyond your comprehension.

When you radiate and LIVE in gratitude, it flips on the ON switch to the universe and it will deliver all the good to you, matching the intensity of your gratitude that is.

HERE IS TO A NEW WEEK AHEAD! EACH WEEK WE START OFF WITH THIS!

The life you want is on the other side of that "stuff" you do not want to do. You have a whole new week ahead of you and though we cannot know what will be in store for us, we can start with a grateful heart and utilize the time we so graciously have been given. With that being said, use the space below to jot down what you aim to accomplish or tackle in the week to come. Do not overwhelm yourself with a huge To-Do List as too much listed is not a good thing. Keep it short and attainable, setting realistic goals.

List 3 things that would help you feel a sense of clarity and accomplishment if you completed them this week.

Make it a practical list of attainable goals so you can check off small wins this week. Instead of an overwhelming project like, "Clean out the garage" try, "Put kids' summer toys in big gray bin and store under the stairs." Remember, it's "progress, not perfection."

To Do's

1.

2.

3.

DATE: ___/___/_____

GRATITUDE » I am grateful for....
(write what you are grateful for and because)

1. _____

   _____

2. _____

   _____

3. _____

   _____

4. _____

   _____

5. _____

   _____

VISION » What would make today great?

_____

_____

_____

_____

_____

_____

Rise in Gratitude • Sheila Chasse

INTENTIONS » Today, I commit myself to....

_____

_____

_____

_____

MAKE SPACE » What is on my mind, in my heart, or on my shoulders?

_____

_____

_____

_____

RELEASE » Let go of....

_____

_____

_____

_____

"One day she realized that life was too short to carry unforgiveness. So, she took a deep breath, let it all go and focused on gratitude for all her blessings instead. She felt so light and free! It was the greatest gift she had ever given herself."

- Anna Taylor

DATE: ___/___/_____

GRATITUDE » I am grateful for....
(write what you are grateful for and because)

1. _____

   _____

2. _____

   _____

3. _____

   _____

4. _____

   _____

5. _____

   _____

VISION » What would make today great?

_____

_____

_____

_____

_____

_____

INTENTIONS » Today, I commit myself to....

_____

_____

_____

_____

MAKE SPACE » What is on my mind, in my heart, or on my shoulders?

_____

_____

_____

_____

RELEASE » Let go of....

_____

_____

_____

_____

"Those with a grateful mindset tend to see the message in the mess. And even though life may knock them down, the grateful find reasons, if even small ones, to get up."

- Steve Maraboli

DATE: ___/___/_____

GRATITUDE » I am grateful for....
(write what you are grateful for and because)

1. _____
   _____

2. _____
   _____

3. _____
   _____

4. _____
   _____

5. _____
   _____

VISION » What would make today great?

_____

_____

_____

_____

_____

_____

Rise in Gratitude • Sheila Chasse

INTENTIONS » Today, I commit myself to....

_____

_____

_____

_____

MAKE SPACE » What is on my mind, in my heart, or on my shoulders?

_____

_____

_____

_____

RELEASE » Let go of....

_____

_____

_____

_____

"Gratitude is not only the greatest of
virtues, but the parent of all others."

- Marcus Tullius Cicero

DATE: ___/___/_____

GRATITUDE » I am grateful for....
(write what you are grateful for and because)

1. _____

_____

2. _____

_____

3. _____

_____

4. _____

_____

5. _____

_____

VISION » What would make today great?

_____

_____

_____

_____

_____

_____

Rise in Gratitude • Sheila Chasse

INTENTIONS » Today, I commit myself to....

_____

_____

_____

_____

MAKE SPACE » What is on my mind, in my heart, or on my shoulders?

_____

_____

_____

_____

RELEASE » Let go of....

_____

_____

_____

_____

"Gratitude gives us eyes to see God, earth, beauty, love, joy, and abundance. Everything we never knew was already right there in front of us, waiting. We just needed gratitude to open our eyes."

- Josie Robinson

DATE: ___/___/_____

GRATITUDE » I am grateful for....
(write what you are grateful for and because)

1. _____

_____

2. _____

_____

3. _____

_____

4. _____

_____

5. _____

_____

VISION » What would make today great?

_____

_____

_____

_____

_____

_____

Rise in Gratitude • Sheila Chasse

INTENTIONS » Today, I commit myself to....

_____

_____

_____

_____

MAKE SPACE » What is on my mind, in my heart, or on my shoulders?

_____

_____

_____

_____

RELEASE » Let go of....

_____

_____

_____

_____

"To the mind that is still, the whole universe surrenders."

- Lao Tzu

DATE: ___/___/_____

GRATITUDE » I am grateful for....
(write what you are grateful for and because)

1. _____

   _____

2. _____

   _____

3. _____

   _____

4. _____

   _____

5. _____

   _____

VISION » What would make today great?

_____

_____

_____

_____

_____

_____

Rise in Gratitude • Sheila Chasse

INTENTIONS » Today, I commit myself to....

_____

_____

_____

_____

MAKE SPACE » What is on my mind, in my heart, or on my shoulders?

_____

_____

_____

_____

RELEASE » Let go of....

_____

_____

_____

_____

"Practice gratitude to honor what's ordinary about our lives, because that is what's truly extraordinary."

- Brené Brown

DATE: ___/___/_____

GRATITUDE » I am grateful for....
(write what you are grateful for and because)

1. _____

   _____

2. _____

   _____

3. _____

   _____

4. _____

   _____

5. _____

   _____

VISION » What would make today great?

_____

_____

_____

_____

_____

_____

Rise in Gratitude • Sheila Chasse

INTENTIONS » Today, I commit myself to....

_____

_____

_____

_____

MAKE SPACE » What is on my mind, in my heart, or on my shoulders?

_____

_____

_____

_____

RELEASE » Let go of....

_____

_____

_____

_____

Grat-i-tude (noun)- the quality of being thankful; readiness to show appreciation for and to return kindness.